Centipedes and Millipedes

By Theresa Greenaway

Photographs by Chris Fairclough

RSVP

**RAINTREE
STECK-VAUGHN**
P U B L I S H E R S
A Steck-Vaughn Company

Austin, Texas

www.steck-vaughn.com

Copyright © 2000, Steck-Vaughn Company

Published by Raintree Steck-Vaughn Publishers, an imprint of Steck-Vaughn Company.

Acknowledgments
Project Editors: Patience Coster, Pam Wells
Project Manager: Joyce Spicer
Illustrated by Dick Twinney and Stefan Chabluk
Designed by Ian Winton

Planned and produced by Discovery Books Limited

Library of Congress Cataloging-in-Publication Data

Greenaway, Theresa, 1947-
Centipedes and Millipedes / by Theresa Greenaway, photography by Chris Fairclough.
p.   cm. -- (Minipets)
Includes bibliographical references (p. 30).
Summary: Provides information on the identification, life cycle, and habitats of
centipedes and millipedes, as well as on how to collect and care for them as pets.
ISBN 0-7398-1829-5 (hardcover)
ISBN 0-7398-2194-6 (softcover)
1. Centipedes as pets--Juvenile literature. 2. Millipedes as pets--Juvenile literature.
[1. Centipedes as pets. 2. Millipedes as pets. 3. Centipedes. 4. Millipedes. 5. Pets.]
I. Fairclough, Chris, ill. II. Title. III. Series: Greenaway, Theresa, 1947- Minipets.
SF459.M54G74   2000
639' .7--dc21   99-37302
CIP

1 2 3 4 5 6 7 8 9 0 LB 03 02 01 00 99
Printed and bound in the United States of America.

Words explained in the glossary appear in **bold** the first time they are used in the text.

Contents

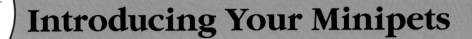

Introducing Your Minipets

If you want minipets with lots of legs, then centipedes and millipedes are for you. They are **invertebrates**, or animals without backbones. They have long bodies made up of a chain of parts called **segments**. This makes millipedes and centipedes appear similar at first, but they are really quite different.

Centipedes have one pair of legs on each segment. You may need to use a magnifying glass to see this clearly. Their bodies are flattened, and they run around very fast, hiding in even the smallest cracks. They are often yellowish or an orange-brown color.

Centipedes

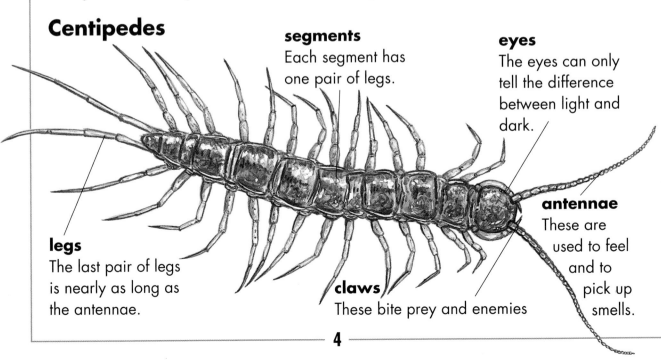

segments
Each segment has one pair of legs.

eyes
The eyes can only tell the difference between light and dark.

legs
The last pair of legs is nearly as long as the antennae.

claws
These bite prey and enemies

antennae
These are used to feel and to pick up smells.

Centipedes are fierce hunters—catching and eating other invertebrates, even other centipedes. The centipede's first pair of legs are sharp, pointed claws that curve forward and look just like fangs. These pinch **prey** or enemies and inject a painful, poisonous **venom**.

Millipedes

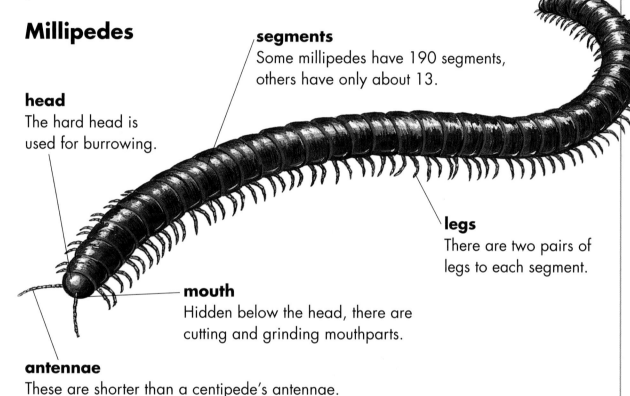

segments
Some millipedes have 190 segments, others have only about 13.

head
The hard head is used for burrowing.

legs
There are two pairs of legs to each segment.

mouth
Hidden below the head, there are cutting and grinding mouthparts.

antennae
These are shorter than a centipede's antennae.

Millipedes have two pairs of legs on each segment. They are often black or dark in color. Millipedes move around much more slowly than centipedes. You will certainly need to use a magnifying glass to look at a millipede's legs. Millipedes eat rotting wood, dead plants, and fallen leaves. They are what **biologists** call "**detritus**-eaters."

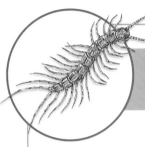

Finding Your Minipets

Centipedes and millipedes can be found all over the world. Most millipedes live in the fallen leaves of the forest floor. But some live on grassy plains, in deserts, and even in caves. Many of the largest kinds live in the warm tropics. Some kinds of South American millipedes can survive underwater when the Amazon region floods.

▼ Millipedes from warm countries are often more brightly colored than those from cooler countries.

Most kinds of centipedes also live in warm countries. Some spend their lives underground. Others hide under stones during the day and come out at night to hunt. There are even a few kinds of centipedes that can live on the seashore.

There are plenty of these leggy minipets in your garden, too. Look for them under stones, in rotting logs, or in the compost heap. When gardeners are digging, they come across them in the soil. Centipedes hate the light. As soon as they are uncovered, they run for shelter.

▶ Lifting up pieces of wood or logs is a good way to find centipedes and millipedes.

Legs and more legs!

"Centi" means a hundred and "milli" means a thousand. Centipedes may have anything between thirty and over a hundred legs, but millipedes never have as many as their name suggests. This polydesmid millipede has around eighty legs.

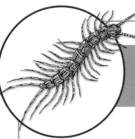

Collecting Your Minipets

Get a trowel, some jars or plastic containers and lids with holes in them, a plastic spoon, a small pot, and a notebook and pencil. Label or number the jars. Now you are ready to start searching.

Use your trowel to dig carefully into the soil. The plastic spoon makes picking up millipedes easy. You will need a spoon and a little pot to collect the much faster centipedes.

Do not use your fingers to pick up centipedes. Remember that even the small ones can pinch with their fanglike claws. Collect centipedes by guiding them with the spoon into a small container. Then transfer them to labeled jars.

◀ It takes practice to catch your pets!

Place some decaying leaves in the bottom of the jars. Put only one centipede into each jar—or the biggest may eat the others. Write down in your notebook exactly where you found each of your new pets.

▲ A centipede hunts for tiny animals among moss and dead leaves.

Pitfall traps are another good way to catch centipedes and millipedes. Sink a plastic container into the ground. Cover it with a flat stone supported by little pebbles. Check every hour or so to see if anything has fallen into it.
◄ A pitfall trap.

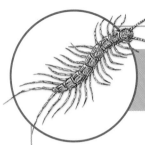

Making Homes

To keep your pets alive and happy, you need to make their new home as much like their old one as possible. Since millipedes do not eat each other, several can be kept together in a large container. Put about 1 inch (3 cm) of loose soil at the bottom of the container, then add a thick layer of fallen leaves. Place a piece of rotting wood and a little pile of pebbles on the soil. Plant small tufts of grass.

You can make the same kind of home for your centipedes, but do not keep too many together at once. The soil needs to be deeper, about 3 inches (8 cm). Put rotting wood and pebbles, or small rocks, on the soil.

grass

rotting wood

soil

pebbles

leaves

Keep the soil and leaves of all the homes slightly moist, but not too wet. You will need a lid with small holes in it for each one. Make sure that your minipet homes do not stand in the full sun all day long.

Backwards and forwards

Garden centipedes hunt in soil or among stones. A centipede has a pair of long **antennae** (feelers) on its head. These help it to detect prey and enemies. To escape from danger, a centipede sometimes has to run backwards. Its back pair of legs are long and trailing. They work just like feelers!

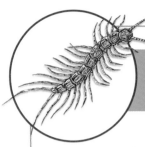

Feeding Your Minipets

Most kinds of millipedes eat decaying leaves and other small pieces of dead plants. Some will eat the kind of things found in a compost heap. But they can be quite fussy and prefer some kinds of leaves to others.

Collect different kinds of dry autumn leaves from the ground under oak, ash, maple, or birch trees. See what your minipets like best. If some of your millipedes were collected from a compost heap, try putting an apple peel, an orange peel, or a slice of raw potato into their home. The next morning, carefully look underneath the food to see if any of the millipedes are under it or feeding on it.

▶ This centipede has killed a caterpillar by injecting it with venom. Here the centipede is eating the caterpillar.

Centipedes are harder to keep well fed, since they need living prey. You should collect tiny worms and small beetles for them to eat.

Have a feeding area of soil or rotting wood that you replace every other day. Your centipedes can hunt through this and feed on the tiny creatures living in it. But be very careful not to throw your minipets away when you change this soil or wood.

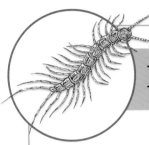

Looking After Your Minipets

These many-legged minipets are not too difficult to look after. Remember to check your notes on where you found them. Then, you can keep their new homes as much like their old one as possible.

Do not let their home dry out. Keep some parts quite dry, but other areas damp. A tuft of moss planted in the damper area will give your pets somewhere to hide. Use a fine spray to moisten the areas you want to keep damp. That way, the centipedes and millipedes can choose for themselves where they want to go. Remove old, uneaten food after a day or so, or it will become moldy.

Top speed

With so many legs, it is amazing that a centipede can run so quickly without tripping. But only one leg out of every eight is touching the ground at any one time. In each pair of legs, one is always moving forward as the other moves backward.

Centipedes and millipedes have poor eyesight. They rely on the senses of smell and touch to find their way around. Centipedes detect their prey by feeling the movements that the victim makes. Centipedes and millipedes use their antennae to pick up smells and to feel their way along. Watch how they use their antennae when they find something new in their home.

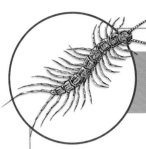

Watching Your Minipets

Centipedes and millipedes are shy creatures that do not like bright light. If they ran around on the surface of the ground during the day, they would be eaten by hungry birds. So the best time to watch them is after dark. Shine a small, not too bright flashlight into their home. Can you see any of your pets searching for food above ground?

Leg work

When a millipede walks, many of its legs touch the ground at the same time. It also has a hard head. This means that the millipede can work something like a bulldozer. Its legs give it a lot of "push," so it can force its way through rotting wood or down into the soil.

Watch how centipedes and millipedes move. To do this, put one of your minipets into a small, shallow container lined with part of a paper towel. Put a clear lid or plastic wrap over the top, or it may escape.

Use a magnifying glass to get a close-up view of it walking. Look at your pet's jointed body as it twists and turns corners and climbs over stones. A millipede has a much more tube-shaped body than a centipede. Do millipedes and centipedes bend in the same way?

▼ This giant millipede is cleaning its legs. It could take a long time!

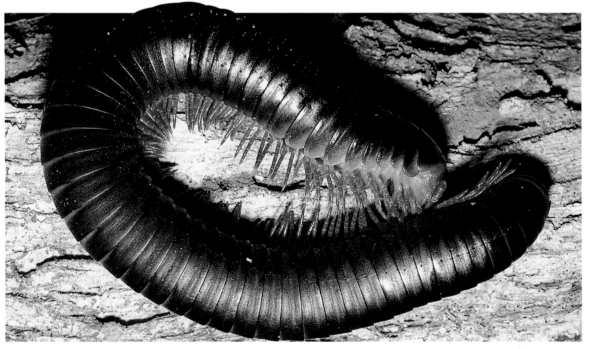

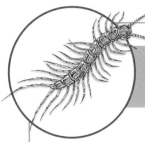

Self-Defense

In the wild, centipedes and millipedes have ways of avoiding danger and looking after themselves. They can hide by running into narrow cracks or wriggling down into the soil. Some kinds of millipedes simply coil into a spiral or roll up into an armor-plated ball when disturbed. Keeping very still can be a good way of hiding.

▲ If coiling into a spiral does not work as a defense, this South African millipede can make an awful smell!

Some tropical millipedes have an even better way of looking after themselves. They use chemical warfare. When attacked, these large millipedes ooze or squirt out foul-smelling juices from tiny holes in their **cuticle**, or outer skin.

These chemicals taste awful, too. To let **predators** know they have this kind of defense, these millipedes have a warning pattern of black and orange stripes.

Centipedes usually rely on the venom they inject with their large front claws to protect themselves. This poison can cause **paralysis** and intense pain in small animals. Long-legged garden centipedes can also shed a few legs if they are attacked. These twitch for a while, just long enough to distract the predator, while the centipede quickly escapes.

Millipedes, lemurs, and terrible-tasting slime

A red-fronted lemur from Madagascar knows that giant millipedes produce a terrible-tasting slime. But these millipedes make a good meal for a hungry lemur.

To get rid of the slime, the lemur rolls the millipede in its hands and dribbles on it. Then it wipes away the smelly slime, often using its tail as a wiper. After that, it crunches up the millipede in its jaws.

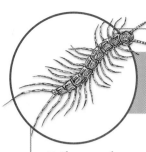

Multiplication

Like other animals, centipedes and millipedes need to get together in pairs in order to mate and lay eggs. If you have more than one of the same kind, the chances are that your minipets may breed.

Some kinds of millipedes make small nests for their eggs by shaping their droppings with saliva. These females may guard their nests. Young millipedes look like short grubs, with only a few pairs of legs. They have to **molt** several times before they look the same as their parents.

▲ These brightly colored millipedes from Venezuela are mating.

Taking care of the young

This centipede from the tropical rain forest is looking after her eggs. She has to keep them clean, or else they will become moldy and die.

Many kinds of female centipedes cover their freshly laid eggs with sticky **mucus**. The sticky eggs become covered by a thin layer of soil. This makes the eggs very hard for predators to find. Because this disguise is so good, the centipede does not need to look after them. Other kinds of centipede females guard their eggs and young in a small underground chamber for about eight weeks. Young centipedes also molt several times before they become fully grown adults.

Keeping a Record

There are about 2,000 different kinds of centipedes and about 8,000 different kinds of millipedes. Of course, you will not find all these kinds in your garden! Identifying centipedes and millipedes can be a bit difficult. Use a wildlife book about your area and ask a grown-up to help you.

Try to identify your minipets, and keep careful notes about them in your nature notebook. There is still a lot to learn about the lives of even common centipedes and millipedes.

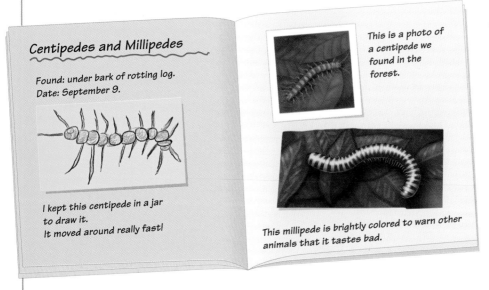

Centipedes and Millipedes

Found: under bark of rotting log.
Date: September 9.

I kept this centipede in a jar to draw it.
It moved around really fast!

This is a photo of a centipede we found in the forest.

This millipede is brightly colored to warn other animals that it tastes bad.

You can create a millipede and centipede scrapbook.

Collect articles and pictures from magazines, and put them into it. If you want to find out more, try libraries, CD-ROM encyclopedias, the Internet, or wildlife clubs for children.

Most centipedes and millipedes are less than 1 inch (2.5 cm) long. The largest are 12 inches (30 cm) long! Sometimes pet shops sell giant tropical millipedes. These are easy to keep, and you can compare them with your garden minipets. But you are safer watching giant tropical centipedes in zoos. The venom of these large centipedes can be dangerous.

▼ Tiny, pink millipedes from the rain forests of Trinidad feed on soft fungi and very rotten wood.

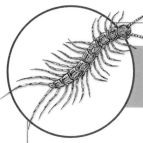

When the Weather Changes

In the wild, centipedes and millipedes may move home when the weather changes. They do not like to be too hot, too cold, or too dry. In parts of the world, such as North America and Europe, where summers are warm but winters are cold, centipedes and millipedes stay alive. They tunnel down into the soil to avoid winter frosts and summer droughts. Deep in the earth, the soil stays damp. It does not get too hot or too cold.

Ferocious hunters
Giant centipedes catch and kill lizards, small birds, mice, and toads. The centipede holds its prey in its poison claws. Then, it chews the soft body with its mouthparts.

On mild summer nights, when the air is damp, many millipedes and centipedes crawl out of their hiding places in the soil to look for food. Some will climb up tree trunks or walls. If you take a flashlight and walk around your garden, you may have another chance to watch and study these interesting animals.

In deserts, centipedes and large desert millipedes rest in burrows and under rocks during the daytime. They might creep out for a short time at night. But when it rains, desert centipedes and millipedes become much more active.

▼ Curled up in its burrow, this millipede is protected from the burning desert sun.

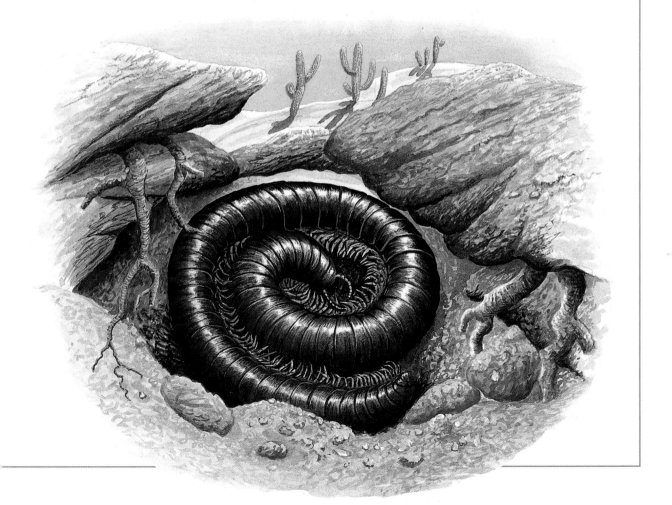

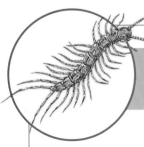

Letting Them Go

One day you may want to let your centipedes and millipedes go back into the wild. It is important to return them to the place from which they were collected. Check this in your notebook if you cannot remember where you found them.

The best time to release your minipets is in the evening, just as it is getting dark. Then they will be able to scurry away before being spotted by a bird. Because they are such good hunters and eat lots of pests, gardeners and farmers are happy to have plenty of centipedes in their soil.

Warning colors

This Indonesian millipede spends most of its time hidden under the bark of rotting logs. If it is uncovered, its bright colors warn predators to keep away.

Most millipedes are harmless to living plants. But a few are not—especially those that like living in heated greenhouses. Do not let your millipedes go free near a vegetable garden. They might damage the crops.

If you bought a tropical millipede from a pet shop, do not release it into the wild.

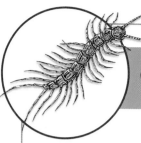

Centipede and Millipede Facts

Japanese "train" millipedes sometimes migrate in huge swarms. When the swarms get squashed on railways, they prevent the train wheels from gripping the tracks!

Pill millipedes can roll right up into a ball when threatened. In this position the millipede's head is protected inside a close-fitting suit of armor.

▲ Even hungry ants cannot bite through a pill millipede's armor plate.

Many large centipedes with powerful venom are brightly colored to warn other animals that they are dangerous. The tiger centipede has orange and black stripes.

◄ A tiger centipede.

The jumping millipede can make a series of 1-inch (2.5-cm) jumps if anything attacks it. To do this, the millipede draws its body up into a hump and flings itself forward in a kind of somersault. Then, it lands facing in the opposite direction.

Centipedes are not really aggressive. They would much rather run away and hide than fight. But if one is attacked, it will use its venom-injecting claws. Only the larger kinds can pierce human skin. But, when they do, the venom causes pain, swelling, and sometimes other symptoms. A baby from the Philippines died when it was bitten by a large centipede.

▲ A giant centipede.

Some kinds of flat-backed polydesmid millipedes live unharmed among ferocious army ants in tropical Mexico. These ants settle in nests for a few weeks. Then the whole colony moves on, eating anything in its path, except for the millipedes that accompany it. Sometimes these millipedes are carried by army ant workers! The millipedes probably act as garbage removers, keeping the ant nests clean.

Further Reading

Coleman, Graham. *Centipedes.* (Creepy Crawly Collection series). Gareth Stevens, 1996.

Cooper, Jason. *Centipedes.* (Animals Without Bones Discovery Library series). Rourke, 1996.

Greenaway, Theresa. *The Really Hairy Spider: and Other Creatures with Lots of Legs.* (Really Horrible series). Dorling Kindersley Publishers, 1996.

Hartley, Karen, and others. *Centipede.* (Bug Books series). Heinemann Library, 1999.

Lowenstein, Frank, and Lechner, Sheryl. *Bugs: Insects, Spiders, Centipedes, Millipedes and Other Closely Related Arthropods.* Black Dog and Leventhal Publishers, 1999.

Parker, Steve. *Beastly Bugs.* (Creepy Creatures series) Raintree Steck-Vaughn, 1994.

Glossary

Antennae The feelers on the head of a centipede or millipede.

Biologist A person whose job is to study animal and plant life.

Cuticle The outer layer of most invertebrate animals.

Detritus Fragments of dead plants and animals.

Invertebrate An animal, such as a spider, insect, centipede, or millipede, that does not have a backbone.

Molt To shed the tough, outer layer of cuticle.

Mucus A slimy liquid produced by some female centipedes during egg laying.

Paralysis The loss of the ability to move in part, or all, of the body.

Predator An animal that hunts another animal for food.

Prey An animal hunted by another animal for food.

Segments The parts into which the bodies of centipedes and millipedes are divided.

Venom Poisonous fluid.

Index

The publishers would like to thank the following for their permission to reproduce photographs:
cover Steven C. Kaufman/Bruce Coleman, 6 Eric and David Hosking/Frank Lane Picture Agency, 7, 9 Ken Preston-Mafham/Premaphotos Wildlife, 11 Harold Taylor/Oxford Scientific Films, 13 B. Borrell/Frank Lane Picture Agency, 15 G. I. Bernard/Oxford Scientific Films, 17, 18 Ken Preston-Mafham/Premaphotos Wildlife, 19 Mark Pidgeon/Oxford Scientific Films, 20 Michael Fogden/Oxford Scientific Films, 21 C. B. & D. W. Frith/Bruce Coleman, 23 Ken Preston-Mafham/Premaphotos Wildlife, 24 Peter Parks/Oxford Scientific Films, 27 Alain Compost/Bruce Coleman, 28 (top) Ken Preston-Mafham/Premaphotos Wildlife, (bottom) Eric and David Hosking/Frank Lane Picture Agency, 29 Oxford Scientific Films.